A
CHILD'S CALENDAR

A
CHILD'S CALENDAR

JOHN UPDIKE

Illustrated by NANCY EKHOLM BURKERT

Alfred · A · Knopf : *New York*

L.C. Catalog card number: 65-21555

This is a Borzoi Book, published by Alfred A. Knopf, Inc.

Copyright © 1965 by John Updike and Nancy Burkert

To
Liz
and
Miranda

January

The days are short,
   The sun a spark
Hung thin between
   The dark and dark.

Fat snowy footsteps
   Track the floor.
Milk bottles burst
   Outside the door.

The river is
   A frozen place
Held still beneath
   The trees of lace.

The sky is low.
   The wind is gray.
The radiator
   Purrs all day.

February

The sun rides higher
   Every trip.
The sidewalk shows.
   Icicles drip.

A snowstorm comes,
   And cars are stuck,
And ashes fly
   From the old town truck.

The chickadees
   Grow plump on seed
That Mother pours
   Where they can feed,

And snipping, snipping
   Scissors run
To cut out hearts
   For everyone.

March

The sun is nervous
    As a kite
That can't quite keep
    Its own string tight.

Some days are fair,
    And some are raw.
The timid earth
    Decides to thaw.

Shy budlets peep
    From twigs on trees,
And robins join
    The chickadees.

Pale crocuses
    Poke through the ground
Like noses come
    To sniff around.

The mud smells happy
    On our shoes.
We still wear mittens,
    Which we lose.

April

It's spring! Farewell
   To chills and colds!
The blushing, girlish
   World unfolds

Each flower, leaf,
   And blade of sod—
Small letters sent
   To her from God.

The sky's a herd
   Of prancing sheep,
The birds and fields
   Abandon sleep,

And jonquils, tulips,
   Daffodils
Bloom bright upon
   The wide-eyed hills.

All things renew.
   All things begin.
At church, they bring
   The lilies in.

May

Now children may
　Go out of doors,
Without their coats,
　To candy stores.

The apple branches
　And the pear
May float their blossoms
　Through the air,

And Daddy may
　Get out his hoe
To plant tomatoes
　In a row,

And, afterwards,
　May lazily
Look at some baseball
　On TV.

June

The sun is rich,
   And gladly pays
In golden hours,
   Silver days,

And long green weeks
   That never end.
School's out. The time
   Is ours to spend.

The playground calls,
   The ice-cream man,
And, after supper,
   Kick-the-Can.

The live-long light
   Is like a dream,
And freckles come
   Like flies to cream.

July

Bang-*bang*! Ka-*boom*!
  We celebrate
Our national
  Independence date,

The Fourth, with
  Firecrackers and
The marching of
  The Legion Band.

America:
  It makes us think
Of ice-cream cones
  And Coke to drink.

The shade is hot.
  The little ants
Are busy, but
  Poor Fido pants

And Tabby dozes
  In a pool
Of fur she sheds
  To keep her cool.

August

The sprinkler twirls.
    The summer wanes.
The pavement wears
    Popsicle stains.

The playground grass
    Is worn to dust.
The weary swings
    Creak, creak with rust.

The trees are bored
    With being green.
Some people leave
    The local scene

And go to seaside
    Bungalows
And take off nearly
    All their clothes.

September

The breezes taste
   Of apple peel.
The air is full
   Of smells to feel—

Ripe fruit, old footballs,
   Burning brush,
New books, erasers,
   Chalk, and such.

The bee, his hive
   Well-honeyed, hums,
And Mother cuts
   Chrysanthemums.

Like plates washed clean
   With suds, the days
Are polished with
   A morning haze.

October

The month is amber,
  Gold, and brown.
Blue ghosts of smoke
  Float through the town,

Great V's of geese
  Honk overhead,
And maples turn
  A fiery red.

Frost bites the lawn.
  The stars are slits
In a black cat's eye
  Before she spits.

At last, small witches,
  Goblins, hags,
And pirates armed
  With paper bags,

Their costumes hinged
  On safety pins,
Go haunt a night
  Of pumpkin grins.

November

The stripped and shapely
   Maple grieves
The ghosts of her
   Departed leaves.

The ground is hard,
   As hard as stone.
The year is old,
   The birds are flown.

And yet the world,
   In its distress,
Displays a certain
   Loveliness—

The beauty of
   The bone. Tall God
Must see our souls
   This way, and nod.

Give thanks: we do,
   Each in his place
Around the table
   During grace.

December

First snow! The flakes,
  So few, so light,
Remake the world
  In solid white.

All bundled up,
  We feel as if
We were fat penguins,
  Warm and stiff.

Downtown, the stores
  Half split their sides,
And Mother brings home
  Things she hides.

Old carols peal.
  The dusk is dense.
There is a mood
  Of sweet suspense.

The shepherds wait,
  The kings, the tree—
All wait for something
  Yet to be,

Some miracle.
  And then it's here,
Wrapped up in hope—
  Another year!

JOHN UPDIKE was born in Shillington, Pennsylvania. Winner of the Pulitzer Prize, the National Book Award, the American Book Award, and the National Book Critics' Circle Award, he has had 35 books published by Knopf, including four children's books. He lives in Massachusetts.

NANCY EKHOLM BURKERT is a Caldecott Honor-winning artist who is well known for her illustrations for *James and the Giant Peach,* by Roald Dahl. A resident of Milwaukee, Wisconsin, she is currently illustrating her tenth book, *Valentine and Orson.*